A dreamer at heart, Nabil Elassi is a bold and creative writer. He loves to wander the world while wondering, his soul in search of mind-bending ideas and methods to speak his truth about the universe we live within. A film graduate, he has worked on several TV programs and writes screenplays for fun, always delving into topics such as life, death, love, dreams, and the universe.

TO FAMILY AND LOVE.

Nabil Elassi

A RED DRAGON'S DREAMS

AUSTIN MACAULEY PUBLISHERS™
LONDON • CAMBRIDGE • NEW YORK • SHARJAH

ISBN – 9789948757931 – (Paperback)
ISBN – 9789948757948 – (E-Book)

Application Number: MC-10-01-2778830
Age Classification: E

Printer Name: iPrint Global Ltd
Printer Address: Witchford, England

First Published 2024
AUSTIN MACAULEY PUBLISHERS FZE
Sharjah Publishing City
P O Box [519201]
Sharjah, UAE
www.austinmacauley.ae
+971 655 95 202

Thank you to those who have influenced me, those I have spoken to, and those I have shared moments with; no matter how impactful or minimal the influence, the conversation, or the moments.

Table of Content

Canvas 1

A Book

A book is a funny thing,
Because if you think about it,

A book is an object,
That we use Earth,
To manufacture,
With the earth's,
Tangible heart,

A book is an idea,
That we once thought,
To write,
With the thoughts,
We were taught,

A book is a message,
That we once believed in,
To inspire,
More messages,
We will preach,

A book is history,
That was once lived,
To travel,
Into the past,
Of a place,
Of a mind,
Of a time,
A book is art,
That is of the conscious,
To admire,
To love,
To understand,
To relate,
To feel,
A book is a funny thing,

Because whether it is,
Right or wrong,
True or false,
We can still consider,
We can consider it art,
We can consider it history,
We can consider it a message,
We can consider it an idea,
We can consider it an object,

A book is a funny thing,
Because if you read from left to right,
You will see it as it is,
But if you read from the right to the left,
You will still see it as it is,
You will still understand it,
And if you read it from front to back,
You will see it as it is,
You will know it as it intended,
When you read it from back to front,
You will feel it as it is,
You will feel it as you intended,
A book is a funny thing,
Because I think,
It is kind of,
Like life,
In some,
Form,
Of a message
Written in a bottle
That is thrown in an ocean.

Karmic State of Flow

One step forward,
Another step forward,
One step back,
Another step back,
One step right,
Another step right,
One step left,
Another step left,
One step down,
Another step lower,
One step up,
Another step higher,

A stumble of steps forwards,
A fall down forward,
A stumble of steps backwards,
A fall down backward,
A stumble of steps to the right,
A fall down to the right,
A stumble of steps to the left,
A fall down to the left,
A stumble of steps down,
A fall down lower,
A stumble of steps higher,
A rise up higher.

To act, will often need a cause,
To act, will always lead to an effect,
A cause can be an effect,
An effect can lead to a cause,
The flow of the waves,
The current of the rivers,
The wind of the skies,
The shine of the stars,
Are at a constant state of give and take,
A simple thought,

May be a cause,
It could be an effect,
It is likely to be both,
Multiply all the causes and effects,
Of the ancients through time,
They echo to the vibrant present,
And will echo into the mysterious future,
Yet the present,
Will one day be the past,
As it was once the future,
And the future,
Will one day be the past,
As it will one day be the present,
Now multiply the souls and spirits,
The ancients, the present, the future,
You will find somewhere,
Between a billion and infinite,
Causes and effects.

For the law of the universe,
Is no simple code to crack,
Nor a simple lock to unlock,
Nor a maze to follow,
Nor an ocean to navigate,
Nor a mountain to climb,
Nor a labyrinth to discover,
Nor a well to take from,
Most definitely, not a well to take from,
Only a well to drink from.

So drink,
Drink with understanding,
Drink with a pure soul,
Drink with honesty,
Drink with respect,
Drink with care,
Drink with love.
Drink until the physical feeling of thirst is quenched,
Do not store its waters for personal use,
Do not try and fool the well or its waters,

For it cannot be fooled,
It will only make you seem a fool,
It may lead you to be a fool,
And even play the role,
Of the fumbling fool.

So drink,
Drink with understanding,
Drink with a pure soul,
Drink with honesty,
Drink with respect,
Drink with care,
Drink with love.

I Am, I Hope, I Fear,
I Be, I Be

I am but a noble translator of colorful dreams into words of black and white.

I hope that someday, bright souls will translate my words of black and white into crystal prisms that reflectively shine all the colors of the spectrum throughout the universe, through a tsunami composed of vibrating frequencies.

I fear that perhaps a conglomerate of souls may imprison my words of black and white into a series of flat, exploitive squares. Or worse, that they attempt to use my colorful words of black and white with the goal of dimming and dulling the bright lights of tomorrow.

I be as I hope,
I hope as I am,
I am as I fear,
I fear as I be.

I be because I be,
I be because I've been,
I be because I'll become,
I'll not become as I've been,
I've not been as I be,
I should not be as I've been,
I should be as I'll become,
If I become as I be,
I will then be as I'll become,
And again,
And again,
And again,
So be,
As you can,
As much as you can,
Using what you've been,

To be as you'll become,
If you become, be,
Be,
Thankful,
Not to me,
Not to you,
But,
Be thankful,
To just be,
So be.

A Nightmare in the Form
of a Dreamy Poem

An argument with my brother,
A reflective glass door like a mirror,
Two sides of the door: one laughing in ego, one raging in terror.
The bull kicks the door in red rage,
The Taurus watches in slowed time,
The shards of glass spread through space,
And all run away with an embarrassed face.

Roughly 168 months later,
Roughly 3 heartbreaks later,
Roughly 440 million seconds later,
In the midst of a lesson from time,
In a state where consciousness determines time,
In the mind of a bipolar, broken soul, counting down time,
The same glass door appears,
Both the bull and the Taurus are on one side;
The mirrored outside,
A muffled conversation flows in like the tide,
It then dies out back into the ocean as though it were indeed a tide,
My ear seems to feel heavy,
The winds are no longer steady,
The sands of time pour out like,
An hourglass with cracks on the top and bottom,
A lesson from the psyche,
I now hear nothing but sand and it felt like cotton,
As I try to empty my ears,
Hitting my head on its sides and rear,
The sand's quantity is exponential,
My mind plotting a plan I deem to be special,
In a sudden moment,
All I could see was darkness,
Was this sand potent?
Blinded and deafened but wary and conscious,
I realized I was not blind,

But my eyes were simply shut,
I tried to open them as one would open blinds in the morning,
But I realized the sun has not risen yet.
Forgetting about the sands falling from my ears,
I could open a single eye but only with the use of two fingers
from each hand,
My brother was standing and staring,
Asking something I could not hear,
I yelled: well I can't hear you because of the sand in my ears,
And I can't see you because my eyelids seem to be a strong
magnet,
One is positive and one is negative,
I then woke up and resumed to live.

10 months later,
Watching a sport I dearly love,
With my other brother and my father,
Lying on the couch,
The first half seemed to be quit the bout,
Waiting during the half time break,
I seemed to fall asleep,
I apparently snored and my brother thought it was fake,
I was awake,
Listening to the poetic commentator,
Wanting to rest my eyes,
My brother asks a question,
I answer.
He then asks another:
Aren't you asleep? I heard you snoring!
I said I'm not asleep, and I was not snoring. My eyes are just
shut.
He was confused and continued watching the match.
I tried to then open my eyes.
But they were shut. Locked. Magnetic.
A moment of déjà vu if I ever knew it.
I had dreamt this feeling before.
I was blind, but it was not physical blindness; my eyes were just
shut.
I could only open one eye with the strength of two fingers from
each hand.

I told my father of this,
He said I am likely to just be very tired.
After 20 minutes of trying to understand what is happening,
My father and brother thinking I have slept on the couch,
I was trying to open my eyes without the assistance of my hands,
To no avail,
The truth was not unveiled,
I finally managed to open them,
Head to my room,
And gave my eyes the rest they apparently seemed to need.

Now I understand that, any moment, is never the truth.
Any moment of time, is but a piece of the puzzle of consciousness,
Any fact of space, is but a tool in the journey of time,
Innocent or guilty, deaf or blind, right or wrong, rich or poor, happy or sad, time will heal all.

High Off of Caffeine
and Nicotine

I LOVE YOU
Caffeine and Nicotine.

The increased energy!
The increased heart rate!!
The increased speed of thought!!!
The increased mental stimulation!!!!

The buzz
The buzz
The buzz

Don't buzz away,
Do buzz into my blood,
Don't buzz away,
Do buzz away from my soul,
Don't buzz away,
Do buzz into these words,

Oh what a lovely love story for the ages!
As simple as any I know to have heard,
I sought you in a time of great need,
You came to me in instant heed,
I sought you when drunk,
I sought you when sober,
I sought you when tired,
I sought you when sad,
I sought you when lost,

Now;
I seek you when joyful,
I seek you when happy,
I seek you when thinking,
I seek you when loving life,
I seek you when writing poems,

Later;
I do not know if,
I will end our friendship,
I do not know if,
I will set safer boundaries,
I do not know if,
I will stay with you,
As you have stayed with me,
As you have entered my blood,
As you have etched yourself in my time,

But I do know,
I will love you forever,
And will always remember you,

But do know,
That I may forget you,

I assume to know,
Not that you will understand,
But that you already do understand,
And perhaps always did understand.

Canvas 2

Red Dragon

I am but a noble red dragon, living amongst many other red dragons, in awe of a green dragon, in the midst of many other dragons, pondering The White Dragon; and it's mercy, mystery, and magic.

White Dragon,
Green Dragon,
Red Dragon,
White Dragon,

First and foremost, the stars and space,
First and foremost, Precise Beauty,
First and foremost, us and them,
Last and not least, Eternity.

For at the birth of the white dragon,
It summoned the beautiful green dragons,
The green dragons grew in number,
Longing for companionship,
Along came the red dragons as a gift from the white dragon,
The green dragons knew at their core, they had the spirit of the white dragon,
However the red dragons,
Knew not that they had the spirit of the white dragon,
In fact, the red dragons know not that they have the spirit of the white dragon.

Through time and in space,
The red dragons war with one another,
The green dragons punish the red dragons,
As though to teach the younger species a lesson,
For the green dragons know of the white dragon,
They respect the white dragon,
They look deep within and beyond for the white dragon,
That is etched within and beyond them,
The red dragons pay no mind,

Some of them know this,
Some of them believe themselves to be wretched leviathans,
Some of them lead others to the white dragon,
But many of them,
Lead themselves and others into using their flames and fires,
To burn down other red dragons,
To leave the green dragons in flames and fires,
But little do they know,
Little do they know,
That in the end,
They only are,
Because of,
A part of,
The White Dragon.

So do not be an enemy,
Be a friend,
To the fellow red dragons,
To the elder green dragons,
And to The White Dragon.

Clouds

An interactive poem where you must listen to the words of the poem as it were some sort of instruction manual to building a piece of furniture yourself. Each line requires one action. Don't worry, they should be simpler than any IKEA instruction manual. The only words that don't require an action, are followed up with a semi colon (;)

Morning;

Look up,
Look up to,
Look up to the sky,
Look up and around the sky,
Notice the blue sky,
Notice the blue sky between the clouds,
Notice the white clouds,
Notice the fluffiness of the bright clouds,
Notice the grey clouds,
Notice the chaos of the dark clouds,
Notice the silver clouds,
Notice the beauty of the silver clouds,
Feel the gradients between the clouds,
Feel the pain of the wisps,
Feel the confusion of the edges,
Feel the depth of the shadows and light,
Feel the context of the contrasts,
Feel the meaning of the shapes,
Feel the lessons of humanity,
Feel the hopes of eternity,
Feel the vision of infinity,
And now,
Smile.

Sunset;

Look up,

Look up to,
Look up to the sky,
Look up and around the sky,
Ponder the colorful sky,
Ponder the colorful colors of the sky,
Ponder the red colors,
Ponder the pink colors,
Ponder the yellow colors,
Ponder the purple colors,
Ponder the orange colors,
Ponder the rays of the sleeping sun,
Ponder the yawns of the waking moon,
Ponder until the colorful sky has transformed into a midnight
blue sky,
Ponder the stars, just for a moment,
As time may get lost in the stars,
Ponder the stars once more,

And now,
Cry.

At the Same Time

Frequently;
I wonder,
Often wonder,
I wander,
Often wander,

That,

She wonders,
She wanders,
He wonders,
He wanders,

At the same time,

Simultaneously,
Unknowingly,
Wondrously,
We wonder,
We wander,
We ponder,
We dream,
We learn,
We think,
We feel,
We say,
We are,
We be,
At the same time,

At the same time,
At different places,
At different speeds,
At different spaces,
For different reasons,
With different situations,
And distinct circumstances

Rarely;
I wonder,
I contemplate,
Wander the mind,
Contemplate the soul,
With the seemingly ridiculous,
Idea,
That,
Perhaps,
Sometimes,
Some thoughts,
Transcend my bubble,
Of my own conscious clouds,
Of our very own subconscious seas,
Of the eternally infinite unconscious skies,

Some thoughts,
Some lessons,
Some dreams,
Some feelings,
Happen to happen,
At the same places,
At the same speeds,
At the same spaces,
For the same reasons,
With, similar situations,
And relevant circumstance,
At different times.

Why Them

Nice garbs,
Luxury transport,
Massive mansions,
A happy wife,
A happy life,
Happy kids,
Childhood,
Dreams

Why then,
Them?
Why them?
Why?
Is it?
Because
They earned it?
They deserve it?
They strived for it?
God loves them more?
They love god more than I?
Or because life hates me more?
Or is it because I hate life much more?
Or is it because I hate me greatly more?
Is it destiny?
Is it dreams?
Is it hopes?
Is it blood?
Is it skin?
Is it pain?
Is it pain?
Is it wisdom?
Is it knowledge?
Is it bravery or chivalry?
Is it honor or nobility or confidence?
Is it grace?
Is it love?

I don't know,
I won't know,
But I do know,
That I could be,
Mistaken to be jealous,
Oh, make no mistake, I am,
Not jealous, not greedy, just,
Suffering,
Suffering with my childhood,
Suffering with my dreams,
Suffering with my parents,
Suffering with my home,
Suffering with my wife,
Suffering with my kids,
Suffering with my life,
That is why I feel,
Hard done by.
Perhaps,
Dreams,
Are my,
Only,
Hope.
I look to their ancestors,
Screaming, bleeding, rotten,
Sleeping a true death I frown,
To think a poisoned apple,
That has rotted many,
Survived many,
Other apples,
Throughout many distant lands,
Has descendants that have ascended,
Through time,
Why them?
They say the Apple does not,
Fall far from the tree.
Maybe, the seeds of the fallen,
Poisonous apple,
Which has not,
Fallen far,
Are,

Planted,
Throughout many distant lands,
Dreaming of holy stands in holy sands;

Their children,
Smiling, pure, innocent,
Living a true childhood, I smile,
To think there is beauty in the world,
My job is to provide safety,
In some sort of way,
To maintain some,
Of the world's,
Beauty.
I one day hope to have descendants,
Who transcend the layers of time.
Not only ascend through it,
And certainly not,
Survive it.
And not,
Exploit,
It.

Black Makes White
Make Sense

What's;
A day without a night?
A sea without a sky?
A tree without soil?
A body without a soul?
A body without a spirit?
A meal without a mouth?
Food without taste?
Music without sound?
Touch without skin?
Sight without eyes?
Life without thought?
Thought without a conscious?
These words without ink?
White without black?
Yin without Yang?
A smile without,
Pure honesty?
Life without,
Laughter?

Black,
Makes,
White,
Make,
Sense.

Remember

A message to me,
A message for,
And from me,
Remember;
This poem,
That poem,
Those poems,
These poems,
Your poems,
Our poems,
Our poems;
Remember,
A message from me,
A message for you,
A message to you,
Remember,
A message from you,
A message for you,
A message to you,
Remember;
A message from us,
A message to us,
A message for us.

Days of Jazz and Soul

Tss,
Dum,
Tss,
Dum,
Tss,
Dum,

Walk awake,
Walk away,
Walk astray,
Walk a day or two,
Walk your shoe,
Walk to who?
Walk to chew,
Walk with food for thought,
Walk a lot,
Walk the lot,
Walk if hot,
Walk till you're caught in your mind,
Walk be kind,
Walk behind,
Walk in blind color,

Tss,
Dum,
Tss,
Dum,
Tss,
Dum,

Walk.

Draw the Color Red
in Blue

Colorizing Colors
Evoking Emotions;

Comet-less Comets
Comma-less Commas
Space-less Space
Timeless Time
Needless Need
Lifeless Life
Deathless Death
Sleepless Sleep
Tearless tears
Fearless fear
Strength-less strength
Brave-less bravery
Soulless soul
Spiritless spirit
Conscious-less conscious
Consciousness-less consciousness
Kind-less kindness
Mindless mind
Starless stars
Treeless trees
Sea-less sea
Sky-less sky
Happy-less happiness
Sad-less sadness
Red-less red
Blue-less blue

Blue-full red
Red-full blue
Happy-less sadness
Sad-less happiness
Mindless kindness
Strength-less bravery
Brave-less strength
Space-less time
Timeless space

Insane sanity
Sane insanity
Insanely sane
Sanely insane
DNA-less DNA
And,
And,
And,
Waterless water
Water-full water
Comma-full commas,
Comet-full stars,
Star-full comets,
Needful life,
Hyphen-less hyphens;

Life full life,
Deathless sleep,
Sleepless death,
Tearless fear,
Fearless tear,
Soulful soul,
Spirit full spirit,
Tree full trees,
Sea full sky,
Sky-less sea,
Conscious full conscious,
Consciousness full consciousness,
DNA full DNA,

Colorizing emotions,
Emotive colors,
And,
That,
Is how,
To draw,
The color,
Red
In
Blue.

Canvas 3

Math Says That:

Value = cost = fee
I believe that:
Value > cost > fee

What's free?
What comes at a fee?
What comes at a cost?
What comes with a value?

What's free?
What is a fee?
What is a cost?
What is a value?

Logic says,
Math says,
The life we live is free,
The air we breathe is free,
The body we move is free,
The souls we meet are free,
The words we speak are free,
The lessons we learn are free,
The thoughts we think are free,
And the struggles we endure are free,

Logic says,
Math says,
A fee,
Is a cost,
A cost,
Is a value,
A value,
Is a fee,

I believe,
A fee,
Is a price tag,
A cost,
Is a struggle,
A value,
Is a dream,

I believe,
A fee,
Is a token,
A cost,
Is pain,
Is torment,
A value,
Is joy,
Is light,
Is love,

Therefore,
Logic says,
Touché,
To the smarter,
To the intelligent,
The douchey bully,
And extremely stubborn,
Math,

Logic,
Though very intelligent,
Wouldn't often admit,
That it is so,
Even more so,
Than it thinks math is so,
It's free flowing and humble ability to,
Use a labyrinth of creativity,
In understanding an idea,
And equations of life,
Allow it to retract,
It's previous,

Statement,
Of fees,
Of costs,
Of values,

And even of,
What's free.

Abstract Love

Read along any row or column, even diagonally, and it will make sense. It will also make sense, if you say it any order as you always choose a connected box. Down to up, up do down, left to right, right to left, corner to corner. So long as one of the four sides and four corners touch another box, read along, a long read, read love, a lovely read, understand all, all will understand.

I	Love	Me
Love	Respect	Love
I	Love	You
Love	Respect	Love
I	Love	Both
Love	Respect	Love
I	Love	Them
Love	Respect	Love
I	Love	Home
Love	Respect	Love
I	Love	They
Love	Respect	Love
I	Love	Her
Love	Respect	Love
I	Love	Us
Love	Respect	Love
I	Love	Places
Love	Respect	Love
I	Love	Lines
Love	Respect	Love
I	Love	It
Love	Respect	Love
I	Love	All
Love	Respect	Love
We	Love	I
Love	Respect	Love
We	Love	All
All	Purify	We

The Chicken and the Egg

Inside the egg,
Is a chicken,
That lays,
Some eggs,
That become,
Some chickens,
That lay,
Many eggs,
And so on,
And so,
Forth.

I Wish

I wish I knew for a fact,
I wish I knew that,
It,
And,
All of,
My wishes,
Would not be true,
But are in fact, true.

I wish.

In the Good

A somber yet chirpy,
Morning,
Believe,
In the good.
My mind demands,
A chirpy morning,
It tells.

A bittersweet feeling,
Believe,
In the good.
My mind exclaims,
A sweet feeling,
It yells.

I try to listen,
But ask if I am to,
Believe,
In the good,
Why do you tell?
Why do you yell?
Just ask,
And I will,
Believe,
In the good.

Yet,
As a logical,
Thinking, being…
I will remember the bad.
I will make a lesson of,
The bad.
But I will always,
Believe in the good.

While

The living,
They cry for,
The dead.
They mourn the.
Dead.

The dead,
Cry for the,
Living.
Their spirits,
Linger and,
Heal the ails,
And screams of,
The living.

The living,
Continue,
To suffer,
In the world.
The dead smile,
In their earth,
Until they,
Remember,
The livings'
Suffering.

They then cry too.
It is,
Up to,
Us who,
Live in,
This world,
To ease,
The tears,
Of both,
Those who,
Live in,
Their earth,
And world.

By doing,
By changing,
By improving,
And above all,
By smiling.

Canvas 4

But a Drop of Rain

It's only,
But a drop of rain.

But it's travelled,
Higher than my body,
Can in a train.

It's only,
But a drop of rain.

But it's pulled,
With the help of gravity,
Without the pain.

It's only but a drop of rain,
But can it travel far?
A simple drink,
As simple as thirst.
A simple journey,
As simple as need.
A simple exit,
As simple as a human body.

It's only,
But a drop of rain,
But I wonder when this,
Very drop, makes way back,
Into the front of a human body,
They say what goes around,
Comes around,
Is the same true,
For but a drop of rain?
For a drop on a train?
Travelling with pain.
Are they tears?
Are they life?
Or are they…
Hope?

For a drop of rain,
Is free and in chains,
It will one day be free as air,
And could possibly be,
As chained as ice.
It still falls with gravity,
Soaring to its freedom,
With hope.
It will be free, despite
The chance of remaining,
In chains.

It's only but a drop of rain.

The Chains of Freedom

Unshackle me!
Unshackle me!!
I said, unshackle me!!
Please, unshackle me!
Please, kind oppressor,
Unshackle me.
We have not walked the park,
In days,
Someone else yelled:
In weeks.
Another exclaimed:
In months.
I heard a wisp of a shiver in the air:
"In Death."

Unshackle me?
I asked,
Unshackle me!
Someone yelled,
Unshackle me!!
Another exclaimed,
Unshackle us,
The shivers said.
I think a moment,
Someone pondered,
Another wondered,
Simultaneously,
We asked,
We yelled,
And exclaimed,
Unshackle us!
Unshackle us!
Unshackle us!
And the chains of freedom
Open up and turn into
Wisps of air,

We look to our oppressor,
Who looks to our
chain-less shackles…
The oppressor runs,
I smile,
Someone laughs,
Another chases him
In mockery,
The wisps follow the oppressor,
And they tell us one last time,
"In Death."

Porcelain and Ceramic

Travelling back to Forever
Running to Nevermore
Dancing to Evermore
Eating till Forever full
Drinking to Always
Balloons, bubbles,
Ponies, a castle,
And happiness.

I would pass by porcelain,
Run on ceramic,
Dance with porcelain,
Eat with ceramic,
And drink on,
Porcelain and ceramic,
Not a heed given to,
Porcelain nor ceramic.

Travel forth to the ever present,
Present,
Running, Dancing,
Eating and Drinking,
To no avail;
Running to eat,
Dancing to drinks,
Eating to run,
Drinking to dance,
I still have no heed to,
The porcelain and ceramic.

It withered,
A granted taken,
Taken for granted,
It spoiled,
Or was I?
Or did I?
Until I,
Until I stumbled,
Wondrously stumbled,
On Porcelain and Ceramic.
I now:

Run on Ceramic,
Dance with Porcelain,
Eat with Ceramic,
And drink on,
Porcelain and Ceramic,
Sometimes giving heed,
I plan to always give heed,
Praise and worth to,
Porcelain and Ceramic.

18 Years, 97 Months, and 5 Days

18;
It took years,
It took 18 years,
It took my childhood,
It ripped my childhood,
It took my heart,
It ripped my heart,
It took my mind,
It ripped my mind,
It took my path,
It changed my path,
It ripped my soul,
It saved my soul,
It ripped my spirit,
It guided my spirit,
It awakened my consciousness,
It killed my consciousness,
It gave me pride,
It ripped my pride,
It built my ego,
It ripped my ego.

97;
It took months,
It took 97 months,
It gave me happiness,
It took my happiness,
It ripped my happiness,
It gave me weight,
It took my weight,
It gave me weight,
It gave me sadness,
It took my sadness,
It ripped my sadness,
It gave me thoughts,

It took my thoughts,
It ripped my thoughts,
It gave me sanity,
It took my sanity,
It ripped my sanity,
It gave me music,
It gave me music,
It gave me music.

5;
It took days,
It took 5 days,
To realize it never took anything,
I am the one who took it all,
It only gave,
It only changed,
It only saved,
It only guided,
It only awakened,
It never killed.
I am the one who ripped,
I am the one who took,
The only thing it took,
Was 18 years,
97 months,
And in
These,
Five,
Days,
I realized it,
Was humbly,
Building a compass,
A meticulous compass,
An intricate compass,
A compass that does,
Not point north,
Nor south,

Nor east,
Nor west,
But everywhere,
And nowhere.
In other words,
It points to,
Love.

Listening to Love Songs with No One to Fall in Love with

To fall, they say,
Without a call,
Towards the sun,
And its bright rays,

To an ideal of the mind,
With a supported wall,
Of the dream of your soul,
Will leave you insane.

Heartbreak, they say,
Will take its toll,
Leave a hole,
That will never again be whole.

Heartbreak, I say,
In all its forms,
Whatever its causes,
Of which not all are love,

Heartbreak beats to,
A very certain beat,
A very certain frequency,
A very certain vibration,

Something like,
The pressure that makes,
A newly formed diamond,
No longer an ordinary stone.

In other words,
Smile,
Sing,
Laugh,
Dance,
Eat,
Drink,
Think.

And never stop,
Don't stop,
Keep going,
Always keep going.

For one day,
One month,
One year,
Forever.

You will,
Love–
But remember,

Always keep going,
Don't stop going,
Keep going,
And never stop loving.

The Slippery Slope

Falling,
Down,
Into,
And,
Onto,
A slippery slope,
At the polar,
North.
Some think it to be,
South.
Falling down a slippery slope,
All there seems to be is a pole.
The pole is in the shape of a line,
Get a grip on the line.
My mind says,
But as my heart drops,
Down the slippery slope,
I realize something,
That could be in,
Itself another,
Slippery,
Slope.
My confidence,
Builds and grows,
Soars and flies,
Roars and flows,
When I realized,
It's fun to slip,
Only in the case,
When you slip,
Down the,
Slippery,
Slope.

Beware of Dancing with Spirits //No Commas

I try to be aware of,
To beware of,
Dancing,
With,
Spirits.
For a tussle,
With a spirit,
Is a tussle with,
Something,
That can be,
Felt but not,
Seen.
But if it can be felt,
It may one day,
Be seen.
For a spirit,
Never leaves,
Never falls,
Never freezes,
Never burns,
Always shines,
And is always free.
If free is what free is,
If free as what free is.

Dancing with spirits,
That are intangible,
Will tangibly,
Tangle,
Your,
Very,
Own,
Spirit.

Awaken the comma,

In time,
The night,
The day,
Might,
Give,
Your,
Spirit,
A gift,
A great gift,
A gift of might,
A great gift of might,
The great gifts of nights,
The great gifts of days,
And a mighty present,
Of presence within,
Your soul,
And your spirit.

I Want to Tell

I want to tell,
But I don't know how.
I don't know if I am right
I do feel as though,
I am right,
But I've felt as though I,
Was right before,
And it drowned me,
It showed me,
It owned me,
It beat me,
It cheated me,

I then thought it to be,
Left.
Then again I felt it to be right.
Then I turned,
Left again.

Felt left,
Alone,
Now I may think,
And feel like,
I am alone,
Though I,
Believe,
That,
I am,
Not,
Alone.

But I felt it to be right again,
For a short while only.
Then I turned,
Left yet again,
For a more short while,

But now I see that all these,
Lefts and rights,
Were on some,
Strange path,
That leads,
To time,
To Rome,
To roam,
To live,
To live,
To love,
To love,
To love,
To amore.

Tomorrow more,
Tomorrow I'll soar,
Tomorrow I'll show,
Today I'll slow,
Today I'll flow,
Now I'll sleep,
For tonight,
So that,
Tomorrow I'll have more,
Tomorrow I'll soar,
Tomorrow I'll show.

I read this,
To hand me,
A hand,
Of comfort,
Of love,
So I,
Can live,
In more peace,
And one day,
Love.

Canvas 5

Just For Kicks

I was blessed with freedom,
At least the illusion of freedom.
I was blessed with comfort,
At least the illusion of comfort.
I was blessed with wealth,
At least the illusion of wealth.
I was gifted a gift just for kicks,
At least it was a gift.
I was happy.
It gave me illusional freedom,
It gave me illusional comfort,
It gave me illusional wealth,
It gave me real kicks,
It gave me real laughter,
It gave me real thoughts,
It gave me real moments,
It gave me real possibilities,
It gave me real opportunities.

Thanks to these illusional blessings,
Real blessings were born,
True blessings were born,
Honest blessings were born,
Fake blessings were torn,
Fake blessings were worn,
Fake blessings were gone.
I was happy.
That was no illusional emotion,
And now,
I am happy,
This is no illusional emotion,
However, this means these fake,
Blessings were likely not truly,
Illusional; they were true,
Are true, as I knew,
I thought them,

To be real,
Even if it were for
A single moment,
Of the past,
Of a present,
Of a dream.

I now know,
That I now think them,
To be real,
To be true,
To be honest,
For eternity.

Identify

Some ideas that have been fought,
Whether wrongly or rightly,
Should be contemplated,
Then assessed,
So identify,
If it is worth,
Being taught,
Being spread,
Before it is,
Force fed,
Into our heads.

Some should be taught,
And discouraged,
Some should not be taught,
Not even encouraged,
Some may need,
Encouragement,
Only if,
It need be,
Encouraged,
As helping a shy,
Soul gain courage,
Is a brave and selfless,
Act.
But remember,
Not all ideas,
Whether good or bad,
Should be force-fed,
Into our heads.
In fact,
Even brilliant ideas,
Don't like being force-fed,
Into any mind,

Just as any mind,
Does not like any ideas,
Enter their domain by way of force.
So identify,
Identify.

All Banks Have Walls//
Do Not Explain Exploitation

How flat is a wall?
How smooth is a wall?
How deep is a well?
How shallow is a well?
How valuable is your wallet?
How much paper is inside your wallet?
How deep are your pockets?
How shallow is your soul?
How smooth is the skin on your face?
How flat is your spirit?
How valuable is your conscious?
How much do you store within your consciousness?
How do you tell this to the time that tells?
How do you pass this to passing times?
How do you reveal this in our space?
How do you shine this onto our space?
Or do you exploit this into our space?
If so, do not tell me, do not tell us,
For space does not need more,
Space does not need more,
Does not need more,
Need not more,
Need no more,
Exploitation.

Through the Shrubs

Sat here at grassland,
As I sit here in the land of grass,
Look through the bushes and shrubs
Look through them by looking at them,
And you will see, that there looking,
Through, is just as beautiful as,
Looking at them. Here at the,
Wonderful grassland.

Look deeper,
Look through and at,
Look inside and beyond,
The path through the shrubs,
You will find that it never ends,
It just spins and swirls and twirls,
Into and onto itself and beyond,
So look at them, here at the
Beautiful land of Grass.
Look through and at,
Look through,
The shrubs.

Sweep

Sweep sweep,
Sweep today,
Sweep all the,
Pain away.

Sweep sweep,
Sweep away,
Sweep the,
Pain of yesterday.

Wipe wipe,
Wipe away,
Wipe your,
Mess away.

Wipe wipe,
Wipe away,
Wipe that,
Which stays like clay.

Sweep hard,
Wipe hard,
Sweep and,
Wipe away.

All the pain that,
Clings to the kings,'
Rings and the social,
Circles mess which grows,
Like cities with buildings so high.

Sweep sweep,
Sweep away,
The class that seems,
To never decay.

So sing and say,
Sweep sweep,
Sweep away,
All the pain today.

Withered Flowers

Wither away,
Wither forth,
Pretty flower,
Dying flower.

Wither away,
Wither hither,
Mighty flower,
Soulful flower.

So wither down,
By flying up,
Up and,
Away.

Wither away,
Wither back,
Dancing leaf,
Drying leaf.

Wither away,
Wither thither,
Lightly o leaf,
Softly o leaves.

So wither here,
Wither there,
By flying,
Down,
Up,
Dancing,
Away,
Everywhere.

Wait

Wait.

I said wait,

I said wait,

The weight of a word,

Wait,

The weight of a line,

The line of a circle,

Wait,

The waist of a circle,

Wait,

The circle of an edge,

Wait,

The weight of a ledge,

To fall or not to fall,

Wait.

The Pearl and the Shell

Peace to all,
Peace from all,
A piece to all,
A piece from all.

The pearl and the shell,
Echo the mysterious mysteries,
Of the ocean wonders and sounds,
To all and from all.

A piece of the earth's soul,
A peaceful soul,
Perhaps not solely at Peace.

But perhaps a piece of,
Mind and the Coral Nerves,
And the oceans cries,
Will lead us to,
The Pearl and the Shell,
In all their curves and crease,
The peace will never cease,
It seems.

The seas will never cease,
The seas may not die,
Not even a Dead Sea,
Can cease to live,
For the Pearl and the Shell,
Not only echo the waters,'
Memories and Wonders,

They Hold,
They Hold,
They Told,
The mysterious mysteries,
Of the oceans:
Wonders, cries, sounds,
Spirits, and echos.

Not only have they Told,
But they have sung,
Not only have they sung,
But they sing,
They tell,
They sing,
And tell till the,
Ocean's Mysteries
Are revealed through
The Pearl and The Shell.

Canvas 6

Walking Truth

As I stand here walking,
As I walk here standing,
I think to the times of my youth,
The times where I could run free,
And others like me,
Couldn't run free.
I could though.

As I sat in my youth,
I could sit standing,
I could stand walking,
I could stand walking,
Others like me couldn't,
I had the luck to gain,
A walking truth,

As I continued to grow,
That luck remained with me,
And Others like me had none
So I gained another walking truth,
Oblivious to the fact that Others,
Like me,
Had no walking truths.

Now, I do not run,
But I have running truths,
Unlike Others like me,
The unlucky Others must chase,
The running truths,
The walking truths,
And even a walking truth.

It is my duty to share with,
The very Others who had no
Opportunities to walk to their truths,
But had to chase and run and suffer,
For their very own truths.
It is my duty,
It is our duty,
The lucky who walked to their truths.

To Hear but Not to Listen

I used to hear,
But not listen.
I heard but didn't listen.
Many used to hear,
And not listen.
Many heard but didn't listen.

I now hear,
And listen,
I hear but do listen,
Some now hear,
And listen,
We heard and do listen.

We do listen,
But to listen,
Is not to do.
As the speaker,
To whom you listen,
To,
Requests you to,
Do.

To listen,
Is to hear,
And to use,
What you hear.
To reflect,
To understand,
To contemplate,
To extrapolate,
To dissect,
To introspect,
To think,
To wonder,

To eat,
To drink,
To digest,
To see what they see,
So you can see what
They see,
Not in themselves,
Not in the world,
But in you.

To see what they see,
In you,
Is but a tool,
Perhaps a sharp tool,
Perhaps a blunt tool,
Perhaps a painful tool,
Perhaps a difficult tool,
Perhaps a magnificent tool,
Perhaps an enlightening tool,
To use,
To grow with,
To fight with,
To play with,
To see with,
To feel with,
To eat with,
To drink with,
To think with,
To hear with,
To listen with,
To dream with,
To live with,
To fulfill with.

So listen.

This May

This may come as a surprise,
But this coming May,
All I hope for is for,
The world to end,
Death and,
Dismay.

Come forth, dear world,
Please let go of any,
Death and Dismay,
On the children,
Suffering and,
Screaming,
And Crying,
And Dying.

Hungry,
Thirsty,
In complete.
And utter agony,
And misery,
And dismay;
Left hopeless,
And in tears.

So this May,
I pray,
That this may,
Inspire,
The earth,
To conspire,
To end:
Injustice,
Apartheid,
Inequality,
And suffering,

For all these,
Innocent,
Children,
Of suffering.

This may come as a surprise,
But as the truth will rise,
It is rising,
And it has risen.
But it will still rise,
But it is still rising,
And it has still risen.
This May,
This may.
I hope.

A Tide

I came from a tide,
I came with a tide,
I was raised by a tide,
I was fed by a tide,
I was taught by a tide,
I learned from a tide,
I learned with a tide,
I grew from a tide,
I grew into a tide,
I was led by a tide.

I was fighting with a tide,
I was beaten down by a tide,
I was defeated by a tide,
I struggled in a tide,
I rose from a tide,
I went against a tide,
I rode south west with a tide,
I drowned in a tide,
I drowned because of a tide.

I flowed north east with a tide,
I learned to admire a tide,
I learned to beautify a tide,
I learned to trust a tide,
I learned to love a tide,
I learned to ride a tide,
I learned to walk on a tide.
And one day,
I will become a tide,
Like no other,
Though there is no tide,
Like another tide,
I hope to create a tide,
Many a tide,
Until a time,

A certain time,
Unique times,
Where tides,
And times,
Meet time,
As a tide.

Know II

I know what I know,
I don't know,
How much I know,
Because I don't know,
How much I don't know.
I don't even know,
All of what I know.
I don't even know,
All of how I know.
I don't even know,
All of whom I know.
I don't even know,
All of when I knew.
I don't even know,
All of where I knew.
All I do know,
Is that I know,
Is how I know,
Is who I know,
Is when I know,
Is where I know,
I don't know what I don't know.
I do know what I do know,
I do sense what I do sense,
I do touch what I do touch,
I do smell what I do smell,
I do taste what I do taste,
I do think what I do think,
I do hear what I do hear,
I do feel what I do feel,
I do see what I do see,
You do what you do,
I do what I do,
We do what we do,
And;
We know what we know.

Ecstatic Mind

I am in ecstasy,
I am in wonder,
I feel beauty,
I feel happy,
I see sounds,
I hear pictures.

But,
I don't trust an ecstatic mind,
As much as I believe it,
For I do not deny,
Its truth,
But I do not trust it,
It seems to be unwise,
Based on my experiences.

For the reasons I do not trust,
The ecstatic mind,
Is not because,
It's wrong,
But on the contrary,
Because I am afraid,
That it is in its rightful state,
Because I sense it is naively and,
Unclearly jumping and bouncing,
Around the realms of time and space,
It is misunderstanding, but true,
It is misled, but confident,
It is astray, lost,
Wandering,
In ecstasy.

However,
A humble,
A humbled,
Ecstatic Mind,
Will see far more,
Depth,
Will see far less,
Grain,
Will hear far more,
Beauty,
Will hear far less,
Noise.
Will feel far more,
Shapes,
Will feel far less,
Pain,
Will smell far more,
Colors,
Will smell far less,
Rot,
Will taste far more,
Flavor,
Will taste far less,
Greed,
And it can even make,
Mathematical absolutes,
Wrong,
It can even make,
2 □ 1

Canvas 7

Know

Do I know?
I don't know,
I do know,
I don't know.

Do I know?
I don't know,
Though,
I do know,
That,
I don't know.

Will I know?
I don't know,
I do know,
I might know.

Will I know?
I don't know,
Though,
I might know,
That,
I will know.

May i know?
No.
May i know?
No,
May i know?
No.
May i know?
No.

Can i know?
Maybe,
Can i know?
Possibly,
Can i know?
Probably,
Can i know?
Not maleficently
Can we know?
Gracefully.

Will we know?
Perhaps,
Might we know?
Unlikely,
When will we know?
I know the answer is:
As unknowable as infinity,
When might we know?
I know the answer is:
As mysterious as infinity.

All I know,
Is,
If we know,
I will let you know.
As,
If you know,
You would let us know,
And in doing so,
Let me know.

Will I know?
I don't know,
Though,
I might know,
That,
I might know.

And if I know,
I will then know,
That I know then,
And then,
I will know,
That when I know,
We will all know,
I truly hope so,
Near as much,
As I hope,
To know,
Now.

Thank You

Thank you,
Thank you,
And I thank you,
And I thank her,
And I thank him.

And i thank my mom,
And her sisters,
And her brothers,
And her friends,
And her enemies,
And her teachers,
And her bullies,
And her decisions,
And her thoughts,
And her opinions,
And her smile.

And i thank my dad,
And his sisters,
And his brothers,
And his friends,
And his enemies,
And his teachers,
And his bullies,
And his decisions,
And his thoughts,
And his opinions,
And his smile.
And I thank my,
Grandpas,
Grandmas,
Ancestors,
And all whom they,
Shared a moment,
Of time,
With.

Whether they,
Spent hours together,
Spent days together,
Spent years together,
Spent decades together,
Learned together,
Taught one another,
Laughed together,
Betrayed one another,
Cried together,
Hated one another,
Rejoiced in joy together,
Loved one another.

Whether they,
Spent but a few seconds together,
Locked eyes while on a plane,
Locked eyes while on a train,
Locked eyes while on a bus,
Locked eyes while on a walk,
Oh, the paradoxical oxymoron.

Of locking eyes,
With another lost soul,
To lock an eye to another eye,
Is the key to unlocking,
The pain,
The knowledge,
The torment,
The happiness,
The struggles,
And the laughter,
Of another soul.

Whether they,
Waited in line together,
Waited in life together,
Waited in strife together,
Waited in light together,

Whether they,
Dreamed together,
Hoped together,
Ate together,
Drank together,
Cleaned together.

Whether they,
Shared a room,
Shared a home,
Shared a building,
Shared a boat,
Shared a village,
Shared a town,
Shared a city,
Shared a country,
Shared a continent,
Shared a world,
Shared a galaxy,
Shared a universe.

And,

Shared,

Consciousness.